Baby Steps H
A Growth Mindset

Author Slimnastic

Slimnastic Community Interest Company

Copyright © 2021

Dedications

Three people have been honoured with this book

All of them have gone above and beyond what I expected

The courageous heart of Kathryn (Kay Yoga Girl), who overcame adversity with unwavering determination

In addition to raising a wonderful family and 12 years of marriage, Marta (Running Woman) Gibek also ran with her baby in a buggy everyday rain or shine

For developing the resilience and fortitude to face life head-on, Dawn Flanagan

I respect and admire motivation and determination

If you possess these qualities, I will do everything I can to help you

Congratulations and keep up the excellent work

Table Of Contents

Foreword

Baby Steps is an enlightening and transformative journey. The book does three things: -

It gives you an understanding of how your brain works

It explains the main factors that influence our mindset

It teaches you practical ways to develop a growth mindset in yourself

Baby Steps is both fascinating, as well as easy to read. You can read it in one sitting or over several days.

I guarantee it will make you think differently about the world - and, more importantly, it will enable you to help you take those first steps towards fulfilling their true potential.

The book was designed specifically for people who wanted to change their life

This book wasn't written to advise people what to do.

Rather, it was to share my experience and how I found my way out of my situation

My background was bodybuilding & martial arts

I have had asthma, since childhood then the unexpected happened i had a heart attack at 40.

After I was diagnosed with further illness, including a vestibular migraine, a hernia, diverticulosis, and type 2 diabetes, I went into depression I put on a lot of weight through the medication I was prescribed

I couldn't walk more than 50 yards without fighting for breath I couldn't function on any level during this time.

My mindset was fixed, and I saw no way out.

Below is a picture of me just before I had a heart attack

Things came to a head one day when I thought I was going to die. The transition from a fixed mindset to a growth mindset takes baby steps, hence the title of

the book You need to make small changes to make a big difference, but most of all you need to be open to those changes.

Over time, I noticed I was making small changes to my lifestyle, choosing to walk instead of taking public transport, checking what I ate, and so on I realized that the quality of my life improved every day after changing my mindset.

To regain my health, I decided to return to the gym again

There were a few things that frustrated me about returning to the gym Personal trainers and gym memberships can be expensive

Some people feel uncomfortable working out at gyms because of their elitist clientele

Training people with medical problems is often challenging for trainers because they lack the necessary knowledge

The cost of gym membership for medically retired people is still too high

After I started thinking about how I could help the people who really need it, I started trying to figure out how I could make a difference

When I decided to enrol in a personal trainer course, A lot of people kept telling me I had too much fat and that I could never be a personal trainer

After completing the level 2 fitness instructor course, I got a certification

Passed the Personal Trainer Level 3 course

I passed the Advanced Trainer course

I passed the Group Exercise Training Course

My next course was the exercise referrals course, which I passed

After which i establishing Slimnastic Community Interest Company, I now offer free training for those in need for one reason or another, I was told I couldn't do it all the way through my journey.

Those who doubted me had a fixed mindset. Those who would rather take the safe route.

My favourite example to use when talking to these people is the dinosaurs. Dinosaurs could not adapt to the change, so they ultimately became extinct

You need goals to move forward, a direction to follow, and a vision of where you want to end up. Additionally, you need to believe in yourself,

"Knock me down seven times and I'll still get up eight times."

While I have a long way to go and I still have a lot to learn, I have developed a can-do attitude in the process.

I always look forward and never backward

Please read the following chapters and take action based on their advice.

If you need advice at any time, please use my website to reach me.

www.slimnastic.com

Everything you need is there.

Anybody who is serious about changing can count on me for motivation and assistance

This is a picture of me at that time in my life. 55 years old bad heart, can't walk far, can't breathe properly

14

3 Steps to Discovering Your Life's Purpose

The question of what our purpose is in life is one of the most difficult things we must face as humans.

Our book will guide you step-by-step through the process.

At the end, you should reflect on your feelings and possibilities. you should have a solid tool you can use to help give your life a meaningful direction

To find your purpose in life, you must go through three steps.

1. **Recognise the importance of the principle of choice**
2. **Coming up with your "underlying principle"**
3. **Using this basic idea to guide your life**

Understanding the Choice Principle

"The most powerful tool we have is the ability to choose"

Norman Vincent Peale.

It is a proven fact that if you've been struggling with sadness, you can choose to be joyful instead.

And by putting forth the effort, you can propel yourself into joy.

When you choose courage, you can overcome your fear. Choices affect the entire trend and quality of everyone's life."

In essence, "choosing" is the most important mental action.

Whenever you do this, you are letting your subconscious know about your wishes.

As soon as your subconscious mind understands your desires, it will do what it can to turn them into reality.

The decisions you make determine your life's goals.

If you are passionate about pursuing them, you have no reason not to succeed.

On the other hand, indecisiveness can not only cause annoyance and tension, but it can also lead to confusion in the subconscious mind over what you want.

However, it is vital that the decisions you make are based on your genuine desires, purposes, and abilities.

It is commonplace for us to allow others to make decisions for us, or to use our belief in what is "right" to decide, even if this means us going against our wishes.

You can only know what is right for you by listening to your heart, and what is right for someone else might not be right for you.

To begin, write down the things you find interesting.

Your favourite things, things that give you a sense of well-being, and motivate you to pursue your goals.

1. **Are you artistic or creative in any way?**
2. **Do you enjoy spending time outdoors?**
3. **Is being by the water something you enjoy?**
4. **Is it a pleasure for you to help others?**
5. **Is it your goal to positively impact the lives of others?**

Developing Your Overarching Principle

Your next step will be to examine your list and look for any recurring themes.

It may be the constant reminder of your contribution, or it might be the influence of giving and receiving love.

Whatever you're doing, try to focus on only one single point.

This will be your 'Mission Statement'. You may have changed because of a quote by a famous person or a thought that has been especially meaningful to you.

As you grow older, this statement will change, but its essence will remain the same.

Now is the time to formulate your mission statement.

Aligning Your Life with Your Priorities

Finally, you must map out your course to reach your goal.

Implement lifestyle changes that help you to align your day-to-day activities with it.

By making these simple lifestyle changes, you can start living the idea every day.

The more aware and intentional you are about this fundamental principle in your life, the greater your excitement for life will be.

Take vacation plans if you find you enjoy being outside. It may be enough to recharge your batteries to spend the day with your kids.

If you enjoy assisting others in need, you may want to look for volunteer opportunities in your town.

Alternately, you may wish to change jobs or start your own business that will help you achieve your goals.

This is all there is to it

By following the steps above, you'll be well on your way to discovering and fulfilling your mission.

"You were created on this earth to achieve your highest self, to live out your mission, and to do it courageously"

Steve Maraboli

4 Tips to Avoid Procrastination

Almost all of us have done it at least once in our lives. The gym is put off until tomorrow; the project is put off until tomorrow; we put off the business venture until tomorrow.

Having procrastination on your side can prevent you from achieving your goals. In summary, there are four approaches to slaying this giant.

1. You should get started right away.

Do not wait. Putting things off until the last minute is an unproductive habit, which is hard to break since it is ingrained in our subconscious mind.

This is normal, and we keep ongoing. In fact, it may even seem strange or rushed to finish a task right away.

2. Don't be afraid to start small.

Procrastination can occur when we are intimidated by the tasks ahead. For example, we may not know where to begin.

Taking things one step at a time is perfectly acceptable in these situations.

Consider the situation in which you're trying to write a business plan and have stared at a blank screen for the fifth time this week.

You may just need to do more research before you start...you are still not ready. The project can be divided into smaller chunks, and each can be worked on separately.

Celebrate and congratulate yourself after you complete each task as a separate project.

3. Putting it off Why are you dragging this out?

In some cases, it may be better to move forward with something you have been putting off for a long time. Somewhere, something is trying to communicate with you. It is your instinct, and it's almost always right.

Give some thought to something you have put off for a long time.

1. **Why did you decide to take on this task in the first place?**
2. **Have you been asked to do this by someone?**
3. **Whose plans, are they?**
4. **What are the reasons for such a long wait for you?**

I'm usually glad I procrastinated every time I put something off.

After procrastination for a long time, disregarding an issue is the last option.

4. Groups that provide assistance

When it comes to big and complicated projects,

Do you procrastinate because you think you cannot manage them on your own?

Do you require assistance?

"Honesty is the best policy"

There is no such thing as an island." Ask for help.

Many resources are available that can provide you with everything you need to complete your task.

When you are a solitary professional who puts off responding to e-mails, do not do it yourself.

You can hire a part-time assistant or recruit students looking to gain experience.

Procrastinating on life-changing tasks may be due to a fear of the unknown.

Consider forming a mastermind group, finding a mentor, and joining a support group.

You do not have to do everything on your own.

Do whatever feels right to you in breaking this habit. There is a good chance you will put off procrastination for a long time.

9 Techniques for Relieving Fear

Fear is one of the biggest obstacles to reaching your goal.

Whether the fear is of failure, success, or something else, fear gets the better of us.

Our lives have all been touched by the fear of failure at some point, and fear can prevent us from accomplishing our highest potential.

Fear cannot hold you back indefinitely if you do not let it. To overcome fear, here are nine of my favourite strategies:

1. Control one's perception of reality

You need to examine what is really happening, then find the facts and overlay them over your emotions.

2. Identify the trigger

Analyse what sets you off about a given situation. Identifying your triggers will prepare you to deal with them.

3. Discover where fear resides in your body.

It is common for fear to control our bodies. Different people experience fear differently.

Determine whether it affects your physical health and take action to overcome it.

Stress can be reduced using stretches, foam rolling, and other techniques.

4. Be Grateful

Gratefulness should be an integral part of your daily life

Every day, choose three things for which you are grateful.

The power of gratitude, no matter how great or small, helps to transform the mind into a positive frame of mind, which eventually defeats fear.

5. Listen to your inner voice

You should check your internal conversations. Make sure what you say to yourself is what you would say to a friend.

You should speak pleasantly about yourself and remember your strengths.

6. Establish a new organization

It is important to remember that the mood and situation will pass.

As opposed to focusing on the scary aspects of the scenario, look at the positive outcomes instead.

7. See the glass half-filled

Perception is a powerful tool, and how you perceive a situation determines how you respond to it.

Therefore, think positively to increase your success chances.

Starting small is the best approach since this is not going to happen overnight.

Are there any negative or frightening thoughts you have regularly?

A good starting point is to reverse the thought. As you practice, it will become second nature.

8. Practice breathing exercises

When you stop breathing, your heart stops beating. Breathing keeps your body in balance.

A grounding practice can be undertaken at any time, or you can simply take five deep, long breaths to relax and centre yourself.

Ideally, you should do this first thing in the morning, but you can do it at any time.

9. Promote a safe environment

When you feel safe and secure, there is no room for fear. Feeling down?

Find a place to go that is safe and calming, whether it is a physical location like your bedroom or an almost mental one like the beach.

As a result, you will feel more secure and be able to face your fears.

Keep in mind that these are only nine options, and not all will be suitable for you.

Nevertheless, this is a good place to start.

Do not let fear prevent you from achieving your objectives this year and begin incorporating these tactics into your daily routine.

6 questions to ask yourself when chasing your dream.

I dentify your objectives and use the questions below to guide you to achieve them.

1. Do you have a life goal that is particularly important to you?

Where do you want to go, what do you want to experience, what do you want to explore, or what would you like to embrace?

If you don't answer this question, you'll have problems reaching your goals.

Intentions without passion will not be able to attract people and conditions that will allow them to become real.

Find out what makes you truly happy.

1. **As a child, what was your favourite activity?**
2. **In your spare time, what do you like to do?**

When your aims transcend your physical self, synchronicity kicks in to guide you.

2. Is this your dream or someone else's?

Are you pursuing your own ambitions or those you're told to pursue by others?

Will you regret not pursuing your dreams in your later years? Is playing it safe something you will regret?

Do you think it's selfish to pursue your own ambitions?

It is impossible to give joy to others unless you have first given it to yourself.

3. Are you willing to accept second best?

In this life, do you feel you'll have to settle for less than your fair share of love, health, and prosperity?

Have you renounced your dream and made concessions?

Nothing can make you happy that prevents you from pursuing your true passions.

4. When you reach your goal, how will you feel?

An individual's enthusiasm fuels their vision. Immerse yourself in the exhilaration and joy of living your dreams.

"Where your creative attention flows, so flows your life," the Hawaiian Kahuna say.

5. Are there any actions you can take today to move in the right direction?

Never give up on your dreams. Develop a plan for getting your goals accomplished as soon as possible and build support around you.

Don't miss out on any opportunities that align with your vision and mission.

How can you accomplish your larger goal with little projects?

Start with a neighbourhood fun run if you want to run a marathon.

Identify options for tracking your progress. Your small victories can be recorded in a journal or shared with friends.

6. Have you ever said to yourself, "I can't have my dream"?

Most people doubt their ability to achieve their goals.

The belief system they follow tells them that they shouldn't do what they love, or they believe they are not worthy.

Dreams are buried so deeply that people forget they ever had one to avoid the heartache of feeling they cannot realize it.

All of us have dreams and every one of us can achieve them.

Why put it off any longer?

3 tips to help you manage your life

There are several simple strategies you can use to stay focused and achieve your goals, from getting organized to making the most of your time.

1. Where do you think improvements can be made?

Even though reality television offers more entertainment than washing the green film from the shower stall, it is not enough to prevent your home from becoming a biohazard.

By setting priorities and adhering to them, you will spend less time worrying about what needs to be done and more time achieving your goals.

Consider reviewing weekly goals and priorities on Sundays when you usually complain about the weekend ending.

This is an effective way to stay on top of your goals and not get ahead of yourself.

2. The Junk You Keep Keeping your junk for too long may lead to it becoming a clutter.

When your neighbours mistake your garage for a garbage dump, you have a problem.

Don't keep old clothes, furniture, appliances, or appliances that clutter your life; consider selling them online on sites such as eBay

Someday, you may be able to park your car in the garage.

3. Make a commitment to become more involved in your community by assigning a position to someone else.

Consider setting aside one day every month to volunteer for charities or events rather than avoiding them.

Non-profit organizations are adaptable when it comes to working with volunteers.

None of these suggestions will work until you include them into your regular routine.

Having procrastinated for a few days, you will find yourself overwhelmed with tasks and unsure of how to proceed.

Change will only occur if you are proactive and give yourself continuous reminders.

Rome was not built in a day.

You might reach some great victories if you know when to approach your goals and persist with your efforts sooner rather than later.

10 Time Management Tips

Get More Done in Less Time Have you ever felt overwhelmed by the amount of work you have to do or like there aren't enough hours in the day?

This will assist you if that is the case!

1. Determine the objectives and strategy you want to pursue.

Identify the short- and long-term goals and objectives you have.

Organize your goals and objectives. Knowing what you want to accomplish (and why) makes it easier for you to decide what needs to be done and prepare accordingly.

2. Focus on your most meaningful goals.

There is a need to identify the areas that are critical to your business to be more productive and profitable.

First and foremost, follow basic principles daily.

In Latin, the word **"fundamentum"** means **"foundation,"** so laying solid foundations is the key to everything else.

3. Put an appointment in your work planner.

This helps you stay focused and reduces concerns about not having enough time.

4. Say No "Teach yourself how to say no.

Don't allow your lips take up too much space in your back." Jim Rohm's

Make sure your schedule is accurate before you start any upcoming project.

Aiming for your goals is important; allowing others to distract you is not.

5. Develop administrative, management, and communication support mechanisms.

Every business or personal situation depends on communication

Take advantage of this by making sure you have the right systems in place

6. Are you doing your current activity to avoid doing something else, or is it beneficial for you?

Ask yourself, "Will I be closer to my goal by doing this?"

"There is nothing so pointless as doing efficiently what should not be done at all," said Peter F Drucker.

7. Delegate responsibilities!

It's tempting to do something yourself when you believe you can do it faster and better.

Think of the future: delegation now can save time later and increase employee motivation, confidence, and talent growth if done correctly.

8. Build on your successes.

When was the last time you took a vacation and how productive were you in the days leading up to it?

To become so focused and effective, what strategies did you employ?

Would you be able to repeat them?

You might also pretend you are leaving tomorrow and plan your day accordingly.

9. Keep a healthy balance in your life.

By creating a formal plan for personal activities, you can find time for your family, friends, and health.

Stress is reduced and energy levels are enhanced by a balanced existence.

Managing your time is really managing your life!

10. Prepare for tomorrow

Put an end to the day by cleaning up your desk, preparing your next day's to-do list, and prioritizing them.

Next morning, you'll be ready and focused since you'll be less worried.

2 Things That Boost Your Inner Confidence

After coaching for a few years, the most significant thing I've learned is that inner confidence is paramount to my success and the success of my clients.

You can improve your life and feel better about yourself through numerous tactics, ways of thinking, behavioural patterns, and practical advice.

However, none of them will be effective unless you have a solid foundation.

This foundation is who you really are because it is who you know deep down.

Finding it and expressing it are difficult because they require confidence.

True inner confidence comes from two elements.

1. Recognize your values

My passion for personal values often prompts me to go off topic when talking about them.

However, I do not apologize for it; it's one of the most important things you can learn about yourself and is crucial to developing genuine inner confidence.

It is your values that make you who you are: they are the building blocks, the foundations, and the cornerstones of your life.

An important value is something important to you in yourself, others, or the world, such as something you believe in, or something you have achieved, or something that is within your capability.

How do you explain your anger, frustration, demotivation, or deflated reaction to certain people or situations?

We perceive it as a negative experience because one or more of our core values is denied, suppressed, or repressed - and it negatively affects us since it denies who we are.

The feeling of being alive, of feeling wonderful, is what I'm talking about.

By living by your principles, you can have more instances in which your values are upheld.

Despite what may happen, no one will take away your values, because they're always nearby, using them is easy since they are never far away.

Once you have a better understanding of your values, you can choose and begin to live your life accordingly.

Simply put, the act of allowing oneself to exist in the real world is incredibly simple, and it feels incredible.

2. Enhancing confidence

In the same way that muscles need to be exercised, confidence must be exercised to remain strong.

It's challenging because your confidence muscle might not be visible, unlike your biceps or glutes, which tend to stay put.

In relation to your biceps and glutes, what exercises do you perform?

Over time, you can achieve the desired results by performing workouts designed to target that muscle.

Self-confidence works the same way. Imagine you are an individual who doesn't take many risks and who simply drives through their days doing the things they need to do and doing them well.

This is without pushing themselves much. As a result of being scared or believing to yourself that doing something will harm you, you may refrain from doing it.

"I don't measure up,"

"Those aren't the things I do,"

"I am not that interested in it anyway."

This type of individual lives within the confines of their comfort zone and what is familiar to them.

The fewer risks they take, the less confident they must be, and therefore the less confident they become.

To build your confidence, you must accept risks, regardless of how minor.

Attempting something new or doing something in a slightly different way shows you are willing to explore new possibilities.

Your knowledge, skills, and identity must also expand as you are open to the possibilities that surround you.

Openness to risk, chance, and possibility will enable you to be more assured, and so you will gain more self-confidence.

How will you exercise that muscle?

Simple by believing in yourself, take a chance on you,

2 Things You Can Do to Boost Your Growth

I t doesn't matter what you do, I have days when I don't feel so well.

The words grumpy, fed-up, and bored come to mind when I'm in that mood, and I'm not the greatest company when I'm like that.

It is an inevitable part of human existence that days such as those do exist.

Bad days are bound to happen, which is normal. If you suffer a string of bad luck that lasts weeks, months, or even years, what will you do?

We often admit that we're stuck, that we're tired, or that we're bored.

We don't want things to stay that way, but we don't know what to do about it.

You lack the energy and motivation to make a positive change when you're stuck.

You can't find the insight or resources you need to make the leap when you're stuck.

Below are two simple yet exciting ways to start climbing your way out of your bad luck and onto a more prosperous and fulfilling future for yourself right now.

1. Take a chance on something completely different.

Life moves more easily when we build routines and systems, but when something runs too smoothly, we become blind to any ideas or choices outside of our routines.

Essentially, everything we do day after day becomes our universe, our whole existence.

Change your breakfast time, radio station, commute route, lunch routine, gym routine, and exercise routine by making one or two small alterations to your daily routine.

Don't stress about whether it's a smart idea; instead, take a few easy steps.

You are immediately pushed out of your comfort zone when you do something unusual or change something about your routine.

You can also let go of things that keep you bound.

You will be able to make fresh decisions, perceive things in entirely different ways, and achieve different outcomes if you break free from your habit.

2. Embrace your instincts

No matter who you are, you have a powerful ally—your intuition.

The dictionary defines intuition as:

2a. Knowledge or perception that occurs instantly, without the need for reasoning.

2b. The ability to see things from a different perspective.

2c. It is a vague or unquantifiable feeling.

You'll never be able to replace your intuition and tuning into it and learning to trust it can work wonders for you.

As with skills like biceps and quadriceps, the development and strengthening of intuition can be similar.

However, it may be harder to detect than a bicep or quadricep, which tend to stay at the same spot.

Here are a few quick tips for accessing it and putting trust in it:

Keep an open mind, be playful, try new things, and don't be judgmental.

Intuition is best developed here. Experiment with crazy assumptions every day.

Try to guess who is calling on the phone, the name of a salesman or a new location.

There will be mistakes; this is just practising that muscle. During your everyday routine, take the time to observe.

You can practice spotting nonverbal behaviour in others in the marketplace, in the bar, or even when shopping.

Pay attention to the ways in which the individual speaks, postures, and eye movements change.

See if you can determine how they are feeling or what they are talking about.

Establishing goals and developing action plans

It's possible you failed to reach your objectives because you didn't create a comprehensive plan of action to achieve them.

Defining goals is only one aspect of goal setting; many individuals forget to make a plan as well.

In the absence of a plan, you will not achieve your goals. It's as if you had a destination but no road map.

A strategy determines how you'll get from where you are to where you want to be.

You can think of a goal plan as a list of things you will do in the future.

It can take days, weeks, months, or even years for these actions to be completed, depending on the type of objective you have set for yourself.

You don't have to create an ideal plan the first time. In most cases, your first attempt to create a target plan will be vague and incomplete.

You won't need to worry; everything will be fine. As you achieve your core goal, you will probably revise your plans as you progress.

Therefore, you must design a strategy that specifies the steps you will need to take to reach your goal.

This involves planning out how you will go about achieving it. Building a strategy is the goal, but the components and what you do with them are the component steps.

If you complete your plan, you have achieved your goal.

It's never too late to create a goal plan. People often take the time to write down their goals every single day, but they fail to develop a real plan.

It is critical for you to establish your goals (your objectives) and create a plan to get there

Besides having a goal plan, you need to visualize your goal to help you put into words what you want to accomplish.

Even just visualizing your goals accomplished before you drift off to sleep will suffice. It will be surprising how much of a difference this makes in achieving your goals if you do this for 10 minutes (or longer, if you wish).

You can easily access your subconscious mind through visualisation before bedtime, which is one of the main reasons it's so effective.

As a result, you'll be able to program your goals into your subconscious, which will enhance the chances that they will be achieved.

Goal setting is relevant for seven reasons.

1. To give life direction
2. To ensure that we, not fate, the media, or others, determine the course of our lives.
3. To inspire
4. Ensuring that we get what we desire out of life
5. To save time
6. To reduce tension
7. To provide a sense of achievement

Although it may be enjoyable to live without direction in the short term, human beings are wired to seek meaning and purpose

Positively impacting the world

I t is normal to feel stuck in life from time to time.

The sad truth is that most people do not have the drive to make major life changes, despite feeling unhappy in their current situation.

Sometimes they do not even know what kind of change they want.

In case a person is unsure of their goals, they can examine all aspects of their lives.

They include health, finances, business, friends, family, hobbies, and their love lives among other areas.

Using a scale of one to ten (ten being the highest), they can rate how they feel about each of these aspects.

After determining which area has the lowest number, they can then consider what they can do to improve it.

If an individual has set a goal (or dream), they may determine the steps they need to take to get there by focusing on it.

It is important to remember that, even though someone's current situation isn't ideal, that is what sparked their goal.

Consequently, it is critical to appreciate where a person is in life in order to cultivate a positive mental attitude.

Having this mindset will allow a person to move forward more quickly.

Being surrounded by people with similar goals is also a smart idea.

By providing support for them, a sense of motivation is boosted and creative ideas for boosting their motivation can be generated.

When an individual fails to reach their goal, it is almost always because they quit before they reach the "finish line."

Sometimes all that is required is to keep trying and not give up.

If you need more motivation, a life coach can help you identify what you want and give you the tools to achieve it.

By using the subconscious mind's potential, hypnotherapists can also facilitate faster goal-achieving with positive imagery.

To make significant life changes, it is highly recommended that people combine the two strategies.

Set and achieve attainable goals using seven steps

The key to success is setting objectives, right? You've heard that a thousand times. Success is more complex than simply setting goals, as you are probably aware.

What does it take to achieve your goals?

I'll discuss why so many people fail to achieve their goals.

1. How would you define a goal?

Defining a goal as a measurable target that can be reached in small steps is vital.

There is a sense of existence to it, more than just a wish or need.

An aspiration or desire is more intangible, ephemeral, and ephemeral in nature. It is impossible not to dream about winning the lottery, right? By definition, a goal is something you want, need, or hope to accomplish. The goal extends beyond just wishing

2. How do you set goals most effectively?

In order to set a goal, you need to identify a need or want you can meet.

Consider the following: Do you know what you're looking for?

Where do you see yourself in the future?

Are you a professional, a student, or a volunteer?

Any action that meets a need, wish, or want qualifies as a goal.

By breaking the objective into smaller, more detailed tasks, we reach our goal.

Keeping track of your progress is essential in setting achievable goals.

The long-term objectives of life are achieved in small and medium-sized steps over time.

3. What steps need to be taken?

Your participation is essential to achieving goals. You must first determine the actions you need to take to reach the goal.

Write down your objectives as soon as possible.

Your goals will become real only when they are written down, so you might want to get a real pen and paper for this purpose.

If you don't write a strategy, you may wind up adjusting your long-term goal to fit your current situation.

Eventually, your desire will become your aim, and wishes are only fulfilled by chance.

4. Review the results

In the next step, you need to examine and plan how you will accomplish each of your goals.

To accomplish each of these goals, you must create a detailed strategy.

As a result, smaller, shorter-term objectives become larger, longer-term objectives.

5. Now that I know what needs to be done, what is my next step?

We encourage you to ask yourself each day,

"What actions am I going to take today?".

The preparations for this week should have been finished in advance, so double check your schedule, and make sure you're sticking to it.

Adding additional processes as needed can be included in the plan.

6. Review your accomplishments at least once a week, and at least twice a month.

Keep a weekly review of your progress.

Look back at the tasks you've completed and those you may have missed.

Adjust your schedule for the upcoming week or month.

The next day, this week, next week by the end of the month, in three months, six months, etc. should always be part of your strategy.

Record your results and keep them in mind going forward.

7. How do you deal with mistakes?

Having a goal means stepping outside of your comfort zone to try new things.

Taking calculated risks is essential to success. It is inevitable that you will face setbacks.

How to Make Goal Setting a Priority

Most people seem unable to navigate their way through life to their desired goals because it is nothing but an obstacle course. In the pursuit of your goal, you will inevitably encounter roadblocks.

There is a need to take action and think things through when these obstacles cause your goal(s) to be put on hold, or worse yet, cause you to abandon your goal altogether.

As a result, here are a few proven tactics for keeping your attention focused no matter what your goal is.

1. Keep a positive attitude

In other words, don't give up. Nearing a goal's halfway point, there is no time for failure.

If you quit, you're automatically back to the start.

That means a lot of time, energy, resources, and money are being wasted.

If you quit, you'll spend more money and experience frustration than if you found a solution.

2. Keep a calm, open, and tension-free mind.

Maintain an open mind at all times. Don't let anything distract you.

Make sure you see the bigger picture and are open to exploring various solutions for your particular issue.

3. Never give up or keep striving.

You should exhaust all options, including trial and error, to find a solution to the situation you are facing.

4. Take some time to experiment.

If there is something holding you back, consider a solution that will help you to overcome it and/or solve it.

5. Ask for assistance

When all else fails, ask for help from those who are more knowledgeable about the task.

Their suggestions might not be what you expected, but they might inspire some creative ideas for finding the right solution.

Your Goals are Within Reach

Overcoming Obstacles One of the reasons we don't achieve our objectives is that we give up when confronted with unforeseen obstacles that we do not know how to overcome.

Whenever our strategies stray from our original plans, we become disheartened, make excuses, and stray from our initial strategies.

Although this is a natural human trait, it isn't conducive to success. To prevent this barrier error, you should carefully define your goals and include backup measures for every possible "what if."

- **What if I do not pass the required course?**
- **What if I am not successful in obtaining the loan?**
- **What if I don't have the time?**
- **What if the marketing doesn't work?**
- **What if I'm just not feeling it?**

All of these are actual barriers preventing us from reaching our life goals.

Our chances of success increase significantly when we plan for them, and by doing so, we become unstoppable.

What kinds of roadblocks should you expect?

1. Internal Obstacles

Negative beliefs about yourself, your objective, and success are internal barriers to achieving your goals.

The most common ones are fears, motivation, self-esteem, and paradigms.

"What if I just don't want to finish my homework?"

Solution:

You should take at least 15 minutes to complete it. Then you can take a break and continue working on it later.

"What if my phobia of talking on the phone prevents me from completing my marketing campaign?"

Making phone calls can be solved by having a friend help me. That means it won't be as bad as it would be if I was doing it alone.

"What if I find myself procrastinating?" you might wonder.

My solution is to have a friend call me every day so I would remember to spend a few minutes working on my goal.

As soon as I wake up, I'll complete my goal.

2. External Obstacles

External barriers include resources, other people's attitudes, money, time, and results.

Our lack of control over them is tempered by our influence over what they do and how they operate.

"What if the client rejects my proposal?" you might wonder.

Resubmit the form once you know why it was rejected.

You can use this strategy for even the smallest goals.

Knowing that when a problem arises, you have the perfect solution for overcoming it and getting back on track is fantastic.

Are You Missing A Key To Success?

Is it difficult for you to achieve your goals at the moment?

Are you able to fulfil all your life goals?

Can you achieve your goals after each success?

Can you always remain calm and patient? Is your lack of progress making you angry, frustrated, and dissatisfied?

When it comes to living the life you want, the answer lies within you. There are two parts to your mind: the conscious, logical half and the unconscious half.

Your conscious mind is what you're using right now to read and analyse these words.

In contrast, the subconscious part of your mind interprets the symbols and helps you decode the meaning.

Mind power is much greater than you may realize, and it can help you in ways you might never expect.

There is a subconscious part of your mind that contains everything that has happened to you.

Emotions and memories are stored in this virtual storage facility.

In the subconscious mind, this is a crucial aspect.

The faster you can access this information, the easier it will be to find your way home, remember names and faces, and accomplish your work; however, there are drawbacks as well.

In addition to storing relevant knowledge, your subconscious mind also stores meaningful emotions. The brain stores, for example, the pain and terror associated with specific behaviours, like putting your hand too close to a flame.

You will feel fearful signals from your subconscious mind as soon as you get too close to a fire and feel its heat.   Secure and reliable, this technique keeps you safe.

Remember when you recently caught a glimpse of a spouse or child, heard music, or smelled cologne and were immediately brought to tears because of deep feelings of love

The subconscious mind can therefore be considered a very basic recording and replay device, like a fully interactive video recorder.

Your memories are a recording of things that have happened in your life that are played back again when you access them.

In new settings, your subconscious mind is likely to access inaccurate or inaccurate emotional memories.

It is common to experience negative emotions or a bad self-image if your subconscious mind has been programmed with these.

Do You Feel Stuck? Think about shifting your focus!

Not only are you not alone if you occasionally feel stuck, but others do too. In an attempt to improve our quality of life, we work, we study, and we try everything we can.

However, it seems that the harder we work, the more stuck we are. Trying this may help if you're feeling irritable...

Consider other people who inhabit this wonderful planet instead of the person in the mirror who is genuinely kind - but also frustrated.

I understand the importance of keeping an eye on ourselves as the number one priority.

In order to achieve our objectives, we should create goals, develop strategies, and then take the necessary steps.

Financial responsibility, making retirement plans, and covering our behinds frequently are essential components of living a fulfilling and satisfying life.

Unfortunately, we tend to become so preoccupied with our own needs and wellbeing that we create large walls around ourselves.

We become unable to see the bigger picture, or even to perceive the opportunities available to us. The ego consumes us so much that we scrutinize even minor events to assess their potential impact.

As a result, we become our own greatest enemies. It is true that we can get so busy that we lose sight of where we thought our life would take us in the first place.

Changing our focus from "me" towards "others" is one viable approach. Instead of becoming a recipient, let's become a giver.

It doesn't mean we should drastically change our daily activities, either. At first, this isn't a necessary step. I'll give you an example.

No matter what you do to survive or keep your family running, you will almost certainly benefit a real person sometime in the future.

Take a moment to consider that. Getting computer systems and equipment up and running is only part of the work we do. We don't just do this to get paid at the end of the week.

Document preparation, assembling electrical gadgets, taking shipments, attending meetings, and so on are just a few of the tasks.

The impact of what you do will almost certainly be positive somewhere, sometime (and perhaps it is already happening). And obviously, if you've been reading, you've noticed that I used two words in the above paragraph - "likely" and "probably."

Since, some people make money by doing things that aren't always beneficial, I had to do that.

We live in a world that works that way.

The work we do and the hobbies we have, on the other hand, often reflect our positive side.

Thus, we return to the first suggestion.

Think about your actions from the perspective of those who will benefit from them. It might help you get over your block.

Considering the ways in which you might contribute your time and talents to others so that they might benefit from your efforts. Can you see what's possible here?

If we begin to focus on "others" rather than "myself," our daily work starts to take on new meaning.

Giving has become a part of our evolution.

The human experience is one of meaning. What we do for others is meaningful.

Can you think of anything more meaningful?

You might want to consider changing jobs - or at least raising your leisure time activities - if you don't see how, you can benefit others from what you do.

Your skills could be beneficial to several people.

Think about your strengths and what you like doing to help others.

Don't hesitate to do it. Within no time, you'll be out of the rut.

Do You Have An Optimistic Nature?

Optimists prepare for a dilemma by looking for positive aspects and brainstorming solutions or ways to solve it.

Pessimists, on the other hand, throw up their hands and exclaim, "That's it; it's all over."

Or they separate themselves from the issue, as if it didn't exist. Denial is an ineffective strategy. Dr. Martin Seligman, the world's leading expert on optimism, says that: we are all born optimistic.

Most adults are pessimists rather than optimists, despite this.

Why is this happening?

The glass is half full for some people.

Other people believe that it is half empty. Do both ideas hold true?

What if it is a combination of the two? People are generally optimists and pessimists at different times of their lives.

Surprisingly, many times, things turn out just as we anticipate. People are usually successful when they think something will turn out well or feel optimistic about something.

The opposite is also true. It almost always fails when someone expects it to.

Oftentimes, pessimists simply say "I can't"

when stressed. Pessimists feel hopeless and powerless, and their responses reflect that.

However, optimists say they won't. They choose optimism overreaction.

Optimists prefer to think in positive terms. In order to achieve what they want, they must focus their attention on what they truly desire, not on what may happen to them.

Take a moment to consider these claims:

Optimists never give up on their dreams, so they succeed.

Success is naturally appealing to optimists.

Optimists are happier, healthier, and more energetic than pessimists.

Optimists inspire others to be optimistic because they serve as positive role models.

Pessimists tend to have more illnesses and live shorter than optimists.

The quality of life of optimists is higher than that of pessimists.

Since optimists have such a positive attitude, even difficult circumstances are not as disastrous as they seem.

In order to be optimistic, you cannot sit back and think positive thoughts.

You can either see the world positively or negatively depending on how you view it.

With a positive attitude, you approach every situation, difficulty, and opportunity anticipating its "benefits".

Your decision will determine the results of your life. Norman Vincent Peale once said, "Change your thinking, and your reality will change.".

It comes down to the fact that how you behave is a choice you make.

When you choose pessimism, you will be unhappy for the rest of your life.

This is because you will see the negative in every circumstance. You will unfairly judge people and see the negative in everything.

What an exhausting existence

In contrast, when you choose optimism, you empower yourself to find the bright side of any situation.

You enable yourself to see the good in people, and to help them see the good in their lives as well. By taking steps to enhance your own life in a supportive environment, you can make a difference in others' lives as well.

The power of positive thinking.

The act of choosing to be more cheerful and optimistic will not make you immune to problems, trauma, losses, and other events in life.

In other words, you will be able to cope with difficult circumstances more effectively. Your chances of bouncing back faster and making better decisions will be higher if you don't let life overtake you.

Take pride in being proactive instead of simply reacting when something happens.

Whether you are naturally upbeat or cheerful is irrelevant. Changing your feelings and attitudes is possible through a growth mindset.

The process won't be easy, but it is possible. There will be some challenging days, but you will succeed.

It is helpful for you to increase your optimism levels in order to enhance your quality of life.

This, however, is not something you are born with. The process takes time.

To become conscious of one's feelings and thoughts, one must intentionally and mindfully be aware of them.

After becoming aware, one must act on what one has learned.

If you ever find yourself thinking negatively, you should stop yourself and try to find the positive side of a situation. Continue doing so until you improve. Your attitude towards life will improve.

As a starting point, here are some suggestions:

Practice being positive and feeling positive.

Open yourself up to experiencing various emotions and novel ideas.

No matter if you're looking for a dream home or a luxurious auto, you can be confident in your ability to attract wealth.

You will achieve your goals by taking productive action.

You should always be optimistic because life would not be enjoyable if you didn't enjoy it.

Keep a positive attitude.

A key to achieving your goals is to eliminate all escape routes. A situation of hardship and obstacles may cause one to retreat into comfort and safety.

If you want to avoid turning around and abandoning your ambitions, you must make continuing forward more attractive than looking back.

It is difficult to achieve a goal if you stick to what you know, what is familiar to you, and what you feel comfortable with.

Upon arrival in Mexico, Hernando Cortez, a Spanish conquistador, instructed his soldiers to burn the ships.

Despite his commitment to his mission, Cortez refused to let himself or his soldiers return to Spain until the mission had been completed.

The removal of this option forced Cortez and his troops to focus on how the operation could be successful.

When the escape route is removed, staying on goal becomes much easier.

The critical point to remember is that, although Cortez ordered his soldiers to burn the ships, he did not order them to burn the food and supplies.

In the same way, cutting off your escape route to boost motivation and inspire persistence when you might otherwise give up is not the same as risking everything.

Planning and management remain essential to achieving your goals.

If you don't plan ahead of time, and therefore lack the appropriate skills and supplies to accomplish your goal, then adding to the risk and stress is not necessary.

Taking risks is both smart and necessary; however, don't be thoughtless or stupid.

Be sure you have all the goods and tools you require before you put fire to your ships.

It may seem that quitting your job is the most effective way to seal the escape route, but if you are short of money, it could leave you bankrupt.

It is possible to take the risk to leave your current career without putting yourself in a dangerous position if you have a savings account or a journey job (a job that serves as a steppingstone to what you really want).

Ensure that you have a strong reason for continuing, and close off all possible escape routes.

Be prepared for risk and have your tools, supplies, and resources ready at the same time.

Despite your best efforts, risks cannot be completely avoided.

Do not rush into things without a solid strategy in place.

Finding Your Higher Self

Tuning into a specific station is as simple as turning on your TV and dialling in.

This rule also applies when viewing specific television shows.

The frequency you tune into determines what you hear and see.

Similar thoughts run through our minds, but we have only two-way stations to choose from: the higher self and the ego.

It is the ego station, which consists of all of our fears-inducing notions of limitation and is associated with the programmed mind.

It is the wounded self, the fake self we were taught to be like children to gain love, to avoid pain, and to feel safe - and it is the ego station.

We are each victim of our own ego injury; it is a closed system that relies on obsolete information acquired as children, information that is no longer appealing or even valid.

It does not readily accept updated, relevant information.

Neither is it receptive to the truth.

The higher-self station connects to the infinite information of the universe, information beyond the grasp of the programmed mind.

As our higher selves, we have access to the Source of Truth, which exists continuously to lead us in the direction of our best interests.

You need to tune your station to it. But how do you do that?

Every person has a dial that lets them tune into either the low frequency of their ego station or the high frequency of their higher self.

The dial represents our intent.

To choose between the two intentions, you have two options:

1. Using a controlling behaviour in order to obtain affection and avoid pain.

2. Embraces the idea of learning and teaching others how to love.

We are bound to our egos because we want to be able to control love and avoid sadness.

When we choose this intent/frequency, we are caught thinking the ideas - the lies - and acting in the unloving ways that cause fear, anxiety, despair, guilt, shame, stress, rage, jealousy, resentment, and so on.

Ego frequency refers to a person's tendency to feel victimized.

Choosing this frequency is the result of adopting the intention to avoid suffering and receive love.

If we decide to learn about what is in our self-interest, and in the collective interest of all, then the choice is ours.

Rather than clinging to our egos, perhaps we should educate ourselves about them.

Choosing the intention to learn about love increases our frequency and gives us access to our higher selves.

We can access the world's information by leaving our home computers' restrictions and logging on online.

Although some material on the Internet may be accurate, others may not be.

However, all information we receive from the station of our higher self is accurate because we receive it directly from the Source of Truth.

Choosing to be our higher self is prevented by our obsession with control.

In order to be in control of feelings, feelings of others, and events, one's ego-mind seeks to be responsible for them.

The desire for control will keep you stuck in the ego station if it comes before self-kindness and living in truth.

As ego stations, we learn that we can exert control over things we don't have control over, such as the actions of others and the outcome of events.

We are given some control over our emotions by addictions, but this simply leads to further suffering.

Taking away our sentiments with addictions just causes more suffering, since our sentiments act as an internal guide that warns us when we're thinking or acting improperly.

It brings immense joy and fulfilment to set the intention to learn about loving oneself and others.

In addition, you can access the wisdom you have when you are tuned into your higher self.

"The pessimist sees difficulty in every opportunity. The optimist sees the opportunity in every difficulty "– Winston Churchill

Taking This Year to the Next Level

It's common for people to reflect at the end of the year and on their birthdays. Here are a few valuable questions for anyone interested in beginning to reap the benefits of self-reflection.

If you need guidance in your life, you can revisit these questions every month, once a year, or whenever you feel the need.

Rather than evaluating your life annually, I encourage you to do so more often. Your life will be more meaningful if you know what you're creating.

As you approach the end of the previous year and the start of the new year, these questions are intended to assist you.

You can end the year strong by addressing these questions so you can make room in the new year for a new "me."

Taking a look back at the previous year:

1. What do I want to be recognized for?

2. Did I achieve what I set out to do?

3. Do I have any goals that I failed to reach?

4. What promises did I make but did not keep?

5. Is there anyone with whom I should maintain contact?

6. Which aspects of my life disappointed me the most?

7. Is there anything I discovered?

8. What are three lessons you should remember this year that will have a lasting impact?

Consider them as a starting point for next year. There is a shift taking place:

1. Can you improve your power by understanding and using your limitations?

2. What is your internal rationale for failing? This is what is causing you to limit yourself.

3. Consider the metaphors that you find limiting.

4. List four elements of your breakthrough paradigm

That you believe will help you achieve a successful future—personal, positive, present tense, clearly defined, and leading to an exciting future.

5. Every morning and before you retire to sleep

Read your revised paradigm aloud. Teach your subconscious that this is the paradigm you want to use.

Looking ahead:

1. What do you consider to be your own personal values?

Is there anything in your life that you consider to be most significant? Is there anything that motivates you?

2. How do you define your life's roles?

Please rate each role on a scale of 1 to 10, with 10 being a priority.

3. Where are you out of balance in your life?

Can you imagine what you'd do if you could solve one problem permanently?

4. With respect to your responsibilities for the coming year, what will be your primary focus?

If you could put a checkmark on any of these roles at the end of next year, which one would you say you're satisfied with your performance?

5. What are your goals for each position?

The idea is that you ask yourself each of the above questions for about a week.

You should be asking yourself these questions often.

The final question you'll need to answer once you have answered all of the previous questions is:

What am I looking forward to achieving and who am I dreaming of being in the next year?

How to develop a life, career, and business vision

Anxiety is a common problem that many people face on a daily basis. I am constantly overwhelmed by all the things I need to get done, but it always seems like there isn't enough time or energy to do them all.

Do you feel this way about your company, your job, or your life?

This month, have you promised yourself you would take some significant steps, but aren't sure what they should be?

You might want to sketch out a concept, but preferably a huge one. This should be a theme that encompasses both your passions and your gifts.

Irrespective of what your business or job is focused on, you have a lot to contribute.

You are unparalleled, and no one else can bring your unique talents to the table.

If you want your dream job, or to raise a family, or even to be the CEO of a large corporation, you have to clarify what you really want.

To get it, you have to take inspired action steps. To help my clients change their habits and concentrate in the right way, I use these exact methods.

To begin, you must be willing to act.

Unless you change your routines and your focus, you will never be able to change the results.

Until you take action, you will never achieve the results you desire.

Coaches seek to understand the client's actual needs and goals and work together to set out actionable steps that will result in success.

It is your responsibility to maintain momentum; unless you elect to receive the support, encouragement, advice, and accountability that a coach provides, you will have to do the work on your own.

Unless motivated and inspiring action is taken, the idea is only a good idea.

One common thread binds you to success in business, happiness and fulfilment in your career, and prosperity and comfort in life.

Vision.

Creativity begins with a vision, a brilliant idea, or a burning desire.

It is these sparks that spur us forward and inspire us to make our intangible dreams become a reality.

Write your ideas down in order to make them real and provide clarity.

When brainstorming, do not edit your ideas or thoughts; let them flow freely.

Identify what you want and how you want to spend your time by starting with your personal vision before moving on to your professional vision.

In doing so, you will be able to identify your life's essentials, your desires, and the things that make you happy.

By building a vision for what you want, you can take steps to make it happen in life.

Be as specific as you can about what you truly desire.

Do more than simply say that you want to make a lot of money, own a luxurious house, and not worry.

Visualize your exact vision, from the carpet colour to the client list, and then create those words until you achieve that image.

Consider the following scenario:

My goal is to run a health clinic that is rewarding and successful.

My ideal client base would include three distinct specializations, in addition to passive income sources.

I work from noon until six o'clock five days a week, and the rest of my time is spent on self-care, gardening, exercising, and spending time with my family and friends.

My salary will be $50,000 a year, and I'll take six weeks off a year.

For the advancement of my career and myself, I spend three weeks every year attending educational workshops and training programs.

In addition to my personal and vision statements, I offer several workbooks, and learning products that provide excellent value and tools to help my clients get back on track.

I find these items really satisfying since they let me earn money without having to be physically present.

It is very meaningful to me to make a positive impact on people's lives, so I strive to do so in my business and community involvement.

Stress-free living for me means focusing on the positive and devoting my energy to the things that really matter to me while letting the rest pass.

Concentrate on what you want to achieve, and it becomes your reality. You create the life that you dream of.

Start by defining your vision; write your dreams and goals for your career, business, and life, and then take action to make those dreams a reality.

It may be a smart idea to hire a coach to help you reach your goal more quickly.

The 3 Best Stress-Relieving Exercises

How do you deal with a situation where your plans do not turn out as planned? Have you ever faced adversity before?

Can you enjoy life when you are anxious?

In order to cope with stress, consider these three tips:

1. Getting more sleep is essential.

Today, most people get less than six hours of sleep each night.

Sleep experts recommend a minimum of six to eight hours of sleep each night.

It helps us rejuvenate physically and mentally.

During sleep, your body is not only resting but is also regenerating.

2. Switch it off.

The convenience of cell phones has increased, but they can also be a double-edged sword.

They are so vital to our existence that it seems impossible to live without them.

The constant presence of news, social media, email, and other distractions makes it difficult to relax.

Before going to bed, turn your phone off a few minutes before bedtime.

3. Consider going on vacation.

It is not necessary to stay at an extravagant resort. The Park or the beach will do, or a few hours at the pool.

Anywhere you can travel without worrying about bills, work, or anything else.

Be sure to give yourself some time to relax! It is impossible to give what you do not have.

About The Author Slimnastic

S ince I wanted this book to be about those who read it and not about me as the author, I did not include my name as the author of this book.

Motivation, inspiration for the people who need it are key aspects of the book

I am not interested in fame or riches all profits from the sale of this book will go to Slimnastic community interest company. Increasing my ability to help others

Sign up and join the mailing list

@ www.slimnastic.com

Follow us on Instagram

@slimnastic

Follow on Facebook

@slimnastic

Shop more products

@ www.slimnastic.com/shop

Sign up for one of our courses

@ www.slimnastic.com/challenges

Printed in Great Britain
by Amazon